LOVE BY NIGHT

S. K. WILLIAMS

Andrews McMeel
PUBLISHING®

Andrews McMeel Publishing
a division of Andrews McMeel Universal
1130 Walnut Street, Kansas City, Missouri 64106
www.andrewsmcmeel.com

Cover Art by Justin Estcourt
Cover Design by Wilder

21 22 23 24 25 RR2 10 9 8 7 6 5
ISBN: 978-1-5248-6119-3
Library of Congress Control Number: 2020946871

ATTENTION: SCHOOLS AND BUSINESSES
Andrews McMeel books are available at quantity discounts
with bulk purchase for educational, business,
or sales promotional use. For information, please e-mail the
Andrews McMeel Publishing Special Sales Department:
specialsales@amuniversal.com.

*for Shayla
for believing in me
more than I ever believed
in myself*

Take me into the night
    The place where no one else can be,
        just you and me

Where our nervous heartbeats
    are the only sounds
and the moon and her stars
    are the only lights around

We will share our fears and dreams
    in equal parts, in equal measure,
and we'll love our flaws and beauties
    in each other and in ourselves

This love will blossom
    into something new,
        something beautiful and true

It won't always be perfect
    but we'll have each other there,
        stumbling together into the dark,
        hand-in-hand until the end

Only in the night,
    we are endless
And only our bodies will ever part

Take me there, into the night

1

35

71

109

143

In the beginning
   there was darkness

and then there was love –
   at least what I thought was love –
   but that was darkness too

and then there were days
   that felt like nights

but the nights
   were romantic,
   lit by cosmic candles
      and the promise of eternity

Night after night
   I spent on lonely rooftops
    waiting for someone
      to share it with,

feet dangling
   over the edge of the world
  waiting my whole life
    for the moon
      to kiss the earth

I get paralyzed by the things I don't know

the outcomes I can't see
of the choices I can't make

possible mistakes

or the leaps I can't take
to unknown lands
with unknown things

Will things change
or will they stay the same?

Will I ever be whole
or only ever broken
and is this it –

or is there more?

There were hard days
    when I felt more broken than loved
    and I thought
    maybe this is as good as it gets

I learned to find my own way
    and there were days
    when I stumbled through the dark

    but I always found the stars

In a garden of thorns
  where nothing can grow
    beneath the thick winter snow

I found you

He and I went out for drinks
    with a couple of friends from work
    and we had such a good time
    it was easy to forget
    the rest of the world

I lay in bed that night
    running things over and over in my head
    the way he laughed
    the way he smiled
  wondering – hoping – wishing –
    I could find some way
    to be the one to make him smile

I want to be – I want to be her friend
One that doesn't have to have an end
   I look at her and wonder what we could be
   Will she share herself with me?

I'm so scared to show her where I've been
   Will she run away from me then?
   I wonder what scars her fingers have felt
   I wonder how many "I love you's"
     her lips have spilled

Will she think that I am odd or strange?
I wonder if she, too, believes one can change
   Will she turn away or laugh if I cry?
   I wonder if she'll be honest or if she'll lie

I don't know if I could
   find the words to speak
I don't know what I'll say if I feel weak
She seems to be gentle, she seems to be kind
I can't seem to get her off of my mind

Maybe this is how a friendship could start
I wonder – I hope – she doesn't
            break my heart

My breath catches when he looks at me
    pulse quickens
    cheeks flush
    my eyes instinctively look downward

This feeling is a sickening rush
I've never thought about him
    like this
        but I am now
            does he know?
        I think so.

He smiles at me,
his eyes linger on me
a second too long
        Does he?
        Could he?

    no . . .

She was so excited to read my poetry
and I was so nervous
journal after journal
page after page
word after word

Would she recognize the ones I wrote
about her?

I don't understand
the heart beneath these wistful fingers –

How did it learn to beat again
when its heart drums were broken?

How did it learn to sing
when it never knew these words before?

How did it fall in love again
when it is still healing from the last time
it fell?

S K WILLIAMS

A lot of people used to tell me
it was depressing

going to movies alone every now and then
going out on a walk to nowhere
          in the middle of the night
going into my books, my words, my head
          to write and escape

but she thought it was beautiful
          and brave
          and inspiring
     no one has ever made me feel that before

Conversations with Myself

He smiled at me the first time we met
   maybe he's interested – he's kind of cute
   but how could he be interested in someone
                          like me?

He waited to leave so he could talk to me
   maybe he wants to get to know me better
   or maybe he's just being friendly

He said he was busy when I invited him out
for coffee
   maybe he really is busy
   or maybe he is avoiding me, maybe I should
                          back off

He agreed to hang out with me
   maybe this is finally it
   or maybe something will "come up"

We talked for hours and it was perfect
   I think he might like me
   then again, *I don't know*

I have always believed
you learn so much more about a person
when you see how they interact with others

    She is so tender to those
        whom others overlook or cast out

    She is slow to judge and slow to anger
        and she listens carefully to each word
          someone tells her
            holding the words in her eyes
            like they are fragile and precious

    She sees the beauty in things
        others dismiss so easily

There is a softness,
   a tenderness about him

He says what he thinks, fearlessly
   but he never means to hurt someone –
   even if he does

He seems to care so much about others –
   not what they think of him
   but how they feel about the world
            about themselves

He is kind to me
   but sometimes maybe not to himself

14

Some people think she's quiet or shy
    but I think she doesn't try to be loud
    she wants to give everyone a chance
                                to be heard

I've noticed the way she talks
    with her eyes
    more than with her mouth

When she's excited and animated
    they open up wide and twinkle
                            with a smile

LOVE BY NIGHT

He reminds me
of the way things were

when I wondered what I
wanted to be when I grew up

when I looked to the stars
and wondered if I'd ever swim among them

when I thought the best thing
in the world
was an ice cream and the summertime
    away from school
    and burying myself in a good book

when I thought all things were possible

and now – maybe again – they are

She reminded me
that it's okay to take care of myself

to fall down and cry and let myself
be picked back up by someone else

to not always be strong

that I don't always have to put
them before me

that it's okay to want someone to
rub your back
run their fingers through your hair
read you to sleep
roll you up into a burrito blanket

it's okay to let yourself
be taken care of

I find myself staring
   at you
   too much

not because of your beauty
   but because
   I wonder if you're real

or when you'll simply
                disappear

Maybe it is simply vanity
　　but there is something in our sameness
　　that draws me back to her again and again

　　It feels effortless to understand each other

　　And I've never known someone else
　　　　who feels so much
　　　　like my own reflection

　　It seems the better I know her
　　　　the better I get to know myself

　　And I don't seem to have to change
　　　　all these things I like
　　　　to make her like me

　　　　　　but instead – she helps me cut away
　　　　　　the parts I never liked about myself

I value my friendship with her
   above my other relationships
   not because she demands all my time
   but because I want to spend
   all my time with her
   because she fights for me when I don't
   fight for myself

The more time I spend with her
the more I realize
   who I was before
   was a whisper of myself
   all the rest of me was shoved underwater
   and was starting to learn to live there
   growing gills to adapt to my discomfort

Her voice is louder for me
   than I ever was for myself

She introduced me to ideas
   I had long ago dismissed
   like
       "you are enough"
       "it is okay to make mistakes"
       "it is okay to be different"
       "you belong"

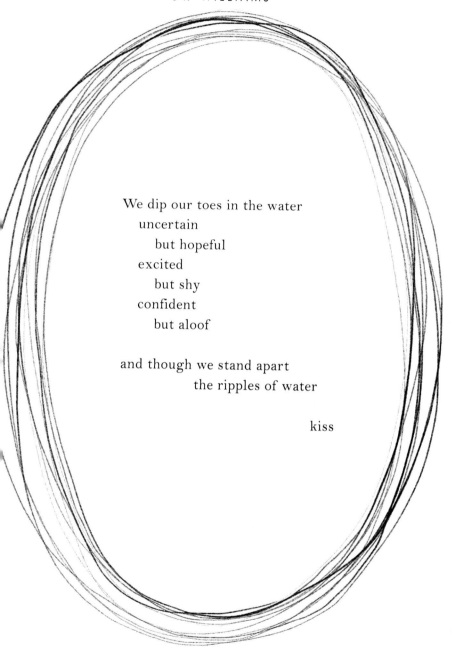

We dip our toes in the water
    uncertain
       but hopeful
    excited
       but shy
    confident
       but aloof

and though we stand apart
       the ripples of water

                kiss

Am I a fool
  for thinking this could be more
    than what it is?
  for wondering
    if he wonders too?
  for letting myself fall for him
    when I don't know
      if he'll catch me?

  for hoping
    against all hope
      he could be
      what I never thought
                was real?

Am I a fool?

I don't know what I was thinking
   maybe I thought if I came over
   I could sweep you off your feet
                       or something

but I'm sitting in my car
   it's been a couple hours
   and I wonder if you'd want me
                    to come in

I've never been more afraid
of anything
than I am
now

of ever losing you

I've never had a friend like this before,
                              not quite

who stays up late with me on work nights
who talks for hours and hours about
    the things we both care about
who holds me when I cry
who lets themselves be vulnerable in front
    of me
who reads the books I recommend
    and the poems I write
who gives me notes back the next day
who pretends like she didn't hear me fart
    and laughs with me when I tell her I did
who lets me be whomever I want to be
    and still values me, no more and no less
who reminds me to take care of myself, too,
    when I take too much care of others
who listens to me and believes me
    when I tell her she is worth it all
who takes my hand when I'm afraid
    and takes the hand I offer her
              when she falls

I've never had a friend like her

Please
   be slow to remind me of my mistakes
   be gentle in telling me when I am wrong
   be kind when you don't feel I deserve it

Please
   remember I am not always right
   and I can't always be strong

You sit
     just inches away
         but the inches
feel like miles
and though we aren't even touching
  I can feel you
  your skin against mine
  the warm smile on your lips
  the wonder in your eyes
  the hope in your heart –
     all the depths of you –
     like an ocean
         unexplored

You tell me
    I don't have to come over
    I don't have to stick around
    I don't have to love you

But you're wrong
    you see
because every part of me
    wants to stay
    wants to be with you
    and wants to love you

    so please
      just let me

There was this moment we shared together
  when it felt like the world fell away from us
    and it was just you and I
    coexisting in this nothingness
And I hoped – I dared to hope –
    the moment could last
            forever

If I simply closed my eyes and believed,

Maybe this would work,
  maybe we could make it
Maybe we have a choice
  and everything that comes after
    will matter more
  than anything that came before

The truth is, it's all a choice we make
  but I look at every possible trajectory
         of my life

And I see you in every direction

I climb back into my car and close the door
your goodbye still fresh on my lips

but I look out and I see you in your own car
    staring back at me
    thinking the same thing

    that it takes everything
        to stop myself
        from getting out
        and getting back into your car
            and kissing you

There was something in your eye
   when you kissed me on the cheek
   and said goodbye
something
   that said
   you didn't want
     to go
   you didn't want this
     to end

Maybe it doesn't have to
Maybe it never has to

LOVE BY NIGHT

You kiss me
   and I'm afraid to show you
      all of my scars

   but you don't flinch
      you don't even blink

You always knew they were there
   but you loved me anyway

Whenever you take me
   by the hand
   and introduce me to someplace new
     it is the strangest thing –

I feel like I've been here before
   and it's always been
     my favorite place

Come inside
take off your shoes
rest your feet;
my broken heart
is open
for you

"I know
you chose me
but sometimes
  I feel unworthy –
  too broken to be loved"

"Maybe you think yourself unworthy
but you aren't;
You are beautiful even when you rain.
Your deep wounds, your cracks, and scars
only provide more places to fill you
with love.

I know you're broken,
but I love all your little pieces
and I love the picture they form
when they come together."

LOVE BY NIGHT

This is different
   He looks at me
   but he sees something more
     and I love what he sees

Together
   we are bigger than ourselves –

   there were constellations
     on our scars
    we'd never connected before

     but together
       we form oceans of stars
         seas of love
        galaxies of tenderness

I love the way
she says "darling"

like it's the sweetest word
she knows

and the taste of it
on her lips
makes her smile

We count down the days until
   we come together
and it feels like an eternity to get here

Maybe this is the day
we quit our jobs and run away
Maybe we are broke
but we'll have each other

I know we both feel it
   weighing us down
     the day is so hard to trudge through
     when it doesn't end in you

I know we can do this
   only just a little bit longer
   push through

I can't get your smile out of my head
I can still see your eyes glistening
   looking into my own
I can still hear your laugh
   and it makes me grin
I can still hear my name
   upon your lips

I don't know where this will go
   but wherever it is
      I'm excited to find out

your goofy laugh
your random cravings
your silly jokes
your honest answers
your passionate tears
your shameless dances
your tender heart
your attentive eyes
your gentle nudges

these are just a few of the reasons
I fell in love with you

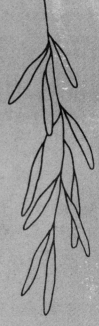

I love the way her mind works

I love the books that she reads
   and the way her mind solves a puzzle

I love the order she brings to my chaos
   and how we find a way to fix things
     when it seems everything is falling apart

I love the way we talk
   both with so much respect for each other
   even when we do not understand
   or think ourselves simply right

I love that she respects my opinion
   and sees me as her equal –
   neither putting me on a pedestal
   nor putting me down

I love the harmony of our minds working
   in tandem
   our mouths – our minds – our hearts
   understanding
yet always seeking to understand better

There was nothing here when you found me

but lights – waiting to be relit
   long grown accustomed
   to seeing in the dark.

But it doesn't matter anymore
   how bad things were before,
   because everything is different now

It never meant more than this
                 before you

You are more than a heartbreak
You are more than broken pieces
You are more than the tears on your pillow
You are more than the scars on your wrists
You are more than the lump in your throat
   the lightning pitter-patter in your chest
You are more than the hole that
    was left in you
    when they left you
You are more
    oh so much more
      than a little poem
        could ever express

LOVE BY NIGHT

She was beautiful
because she had scars
where they had none

because she kept on fighting
when the others were done

because she drank in the moon
while they basked in the sun

When I see you look at me
I can't help but feel more beautiful
I can't help but see my potential
I can't help but like myself a little more

When I see you look at me
I want to be more
I want to see more
I want to do more

When I see you look at me
I see myself too

You make me feel like I'm unstoppable
and when I have gone too far
and remind myself that I'm not
you don't hold it over me

You help me heal and remind me that
it's okay to not be able to fix everything

You make me feel humble and whole

Where is this love?

Painted on the clouds
Hidden in the cracks on the sidewalk
Flickering in the night sky
Behind a subtle smile
Whispered by the wind in the trees

For our first date
she took me to see the otters

We fed them little bits of fish
and watched them squeak and squabble
and chew their squishy food in their
sharp little teeth

They played tug-of-war with a handkerchief
and burrowed their furry little faces
into our cardigans and sweaters
and fixated on her shoelaces
which they were quite adept at untying

and when playtime grew too tiresome
they flopped on their backs into their beds
and gathered little marbles on their bellies
swiping more from our hands
    when we offered them
sleepily fighting to stay awake
to spend just a little bit longer together
cuddling up against each other

their life bond unbreakable

I knew then in that moment
I wanted that with her too

I want to walk the streets you
    grew up walking
I want to see the windows you
    peered out when you were little
I want to eat the candy bar you
    would get on your way home from school
I want to know who you were
    on your way to me
I want to know all the parts of you
    that will soon become a part of me

We shared cups of coffee
  and shows and movies
  and sweaters when one of us grew cold

Little by little,
pieces of ourselves collected into
something bigger

We shared tears and hugs and kisses
  and glasses of wine and plates of torte

Little by little, we grew fonder of each other
  the way humans grow fond of air
  and food and water and sleep

The more we gave each other
  the bigger this all became
  and the bigger it grew
    the more nervous we grew too

Little by little, we began to trust each other
  until we realized
    we didn't have to be afraid anymore
    because we would never take
    from each other,
      only give, and give, and give

LOVE BY NIGHT

I just left your place
and I'm driving home
   but it feels like I'm headed
       away from it

    My eyes wander to the skies
    and though I wish your hand
      was here to hold

    the moon and her stars are out
     never too far from me

    like these thoughts of you
still drifting through the space of my head

I miss you
    more than I've ever missed anybody

    because when you are not here
    I feel like I've wandered outside
                       my own skin
    and everything feels hot and bitter
    and empty and foreign

Now that I've had a taste of your presence,
being without it feels impossibly unbearable

    and I don't know how I did it before
    but I never want to do it again

LOVE BY NIGHT

I could fall asleep
    to your soothing voice in my ears
    over the phone
    telling me tenderly how you feel

All that I want is your arms
    around me
    to ease me into the darkness –
    to take my hand and
    wade with me into my dreams

I want to feel your face in the dark
    but I can't, not yet
    so your words will have to do
                   for now

She told me,
"Count the stars until you fall asleep."

I said,
"There are too many to count.
But I will try."

I couldn't sleep for a week
but I'm still counting
every night

I don't know how many mornings
   I stared myself down
     in the mirror
     picking myself apart;

   pock-marked skin,
   crooked teeth,
   violet bags beneath my eyes,
   lines of stress cut across my face,

        "I never noticed,"
           she said
        "I see all of you, my dear:
        soft and gentle skin,
        the most lovely smile,
        the kindest eyes
        always looking up."

There were things you saw
   that I never noticed

   There were parts of me
     you explored
   that I didn't even know were
       parts of me

He began to share pieces of himself with me
he didn't even realize he was sharing

    the way his eyes lit up
        when he was talking about something
           he loved
    the way he talked to our pets
        when he didn't realize I was watching
    the way he cleaned up after me
        without keeping score or being bitter –
          just because he cares
          just because he wanted to help

I could do this with him
I could do this forever

The stress of the day
pulls me to pieces in every direction

I don't know how to make this work
   how to make time for everything
   how to make them all happy

I wish I could grab hold of the world
 and stop it from turning
I wish I could take your hand
    and disappear

Take my hand
and let me lead you to sunnier meadows
    to happier places

I promise we will get through this
I know your body grows weary
 and your feet are aching
  but I am here to walk beside you
  to take you where you want to be
    I'll be strong for you
    if you'll be strong for me

There is room in my life for you
   it might be a tight squeeze
   but there is a you-shaped hole
      in my heart
   you will fit in perfectly

and if it's too cramped
we'll open things up a bit
   tear down the walls
   and knock out the ceiling
     so we can see the stars
     and give you room to breathe

We went wherever we could
   parks after dark
   the cozy little Italian café
   and there were those nights
     we just drove
      fingers interlaced

Just to be together
   was enough

And some nights
   we didn't need to say
    a word —

      we let our hearts
      do the talking
         instead

LOVE BY NIGHT

We got so caught up in each other, we forgot
   there were other people in the world

We talked about things
   I'd never thought about

We shared our dreams
   and our fears alike

We talked about children
   and how we might name them

We exchanged ghost stories
   we didn't know if we believed in

We talked about who we were
   and who we wanted to be

We learned more about each other
   and more about ourselves
        and the hours
        turned to days
        and we parted ways
            mouths sore
            and eyes weary
            but hearts happy

I know everything between us is exciting
    because it's new
    but this is something more

I want to open a map
    and point out all the places we will go
I want to go camping
    even in the rain
    and lie with you in the grass
    to stare at the stars
I want to take you to places
    that I've never been

I want to make every place
    our place
I want to make a world with you
I want to plant seeds in your heart

Everything's for Sale

I think about this far too much
lying in bed, unable to sleep
   staring about my room:

How much could I get for my computer –
           my bed – my books?

If I got rid of it all
   how much would we have?

   How far would that get us?

   Could we make it last
     until we find something
      we can do
      to pay the bills

   Is it enough?

   Why don't we just
               go?

S K WILLIAMS

Little snowy flurries
　　fluttering down from the icy night sky,
　　the burn of whiskey at our throats,
　　　all smiles and hands —
we couldn't keep our eyes off each other
　　That was when I truly saw you
　　　and saw that you saw me too

Wild, young love
so sweet and gentle
but passionate and raw

We were entangled
   looking for any excuse
   for affection

    and any way
      to run away together

        wild and sweet
          and tender
          and true

    I hope it's enough
      to bloom

Skin against skin
fingers between fingers
arms draped over arms
sweat soaking into sweat
lips tasting lips
bodies emptied
    heavy breaths fill the air

Tangled forms tied together
    locked in love
shapes formed with tenderness
    against the darkness
sweet and wild
    and we are left breathless
        arms in arms
        lips on lips
          love and love

If your eyes made me fall in love with you
it was your hands that made me trust you

They found my own when I was shaking
    and pulled me forward when I didn't have
    the strength to lead myself
They were never cruel nor hard –
        only ever soft and kind

I retreat to them
when every place else in the world is hostile

      Your hand is the safest place
      I've ever known

You trust me
   with the things
      you don't trust yourself with
You treat me
   better than
      you treat yourself
You love me
   in all the ways
      you can't love yourself

Maybe someday
   we can see ourselves
      the way we see each other

She
    makes forever more than a word
    makes tomorrow something to
       look forward to
    makes meaning from nothing
    makes the moon magic
    makes everything the way it should be
       the way it was always meant to be

She is darkness
    and light

       and everything in between

He
   knows just what to say to make me okay
   knows how to hold me tight
     and tell me everything will be alright
   knows how to show me he loves me
    in all the little ways
    I never knew mattered
   knows the color I like my coffee
   knows how I like to be wrapped up
    like a blanket burrito

He is everything
   I never knew that I needed
    and I can never ever
            do without

I want to do more
   than make it from day to day
   than close my eyes and steel myself
   than shut out the voices saying
     "you aren't good enough"

I want to do more
   than this

I want to cross oceans
   dance among the stars
   and have dinner by candlelight
     on mountaintops

I want it all
   and I'm so sick of anything less

I don't dance much,
  but with you
    I have just enough courage
      in the kitchen,
        when the right song comes on,
          and nobody else is around

I don't cook much,
  but with you
    I'll peel every potato,
      shred every block of cheese,
        and wash every dish
          when we're through

I don't sleep much,
  but I think I could
    fall asleep next to you,
      into deep dreams
        where I can be again
          with you

I don't need much
  but I really need you

There will be those hard days and nights
we spend apart
    when the only part of us together
                      is our heart

I will still be there when you wake
I will still leave you notes in secret places
I will still love you from afar

It is a comfort
    that when we are missing each other
      even miles apart
    we both look to the skies at night
      and see the same stars

I find you in the songs
I find you in the trees and all the little leaves
I find you in the words of everything I write
I find you in the beads about my wrist
I find you in the sweet smells of flowers
I find you in the tender glow of the moon

   And I find you in my loneliness
      where only your kind words and
      splendid memories
         keep me going on to brave the
                           emptiness –

      the time we are apart

Your clothes are bigger than me
but they fit just right

your pillow smells a little like you
but a little's not quite enough

your laugh makes me smile
but I need your lips right now

your arms hold me up like the world
but without you here, I'm crumbling

come back to me
when you can
because this life is just too hard
                    without you

How many nights will we stay up all night
   lying in bed
   talking to each other
   about anything and everything?

How many nights will we stare at each other
   until sleep takes us in
   and we fade to dreams
   with our hands blindly clasped
                tight together?

How many nights will we spend
   in these four walls
before we take ourselves somewhere better
where we know we belong?

How many nights will we share together?

I hope there are too many to ever know
                their number.

Laughter wore us down
   our mouths grew sore
   and our eyes impatiently tired

but every ache is lovely
and I'm not ready to fall asleep
weary but not yet ready —
       to let you go from my eyes

Night Beasts

Our clothes hung from lamps
    and backs of desk chairs
        turned away from us

Our drinks at the edges of the nightstands
    absent from our hungry eyes

        feasting on each other

        spent

        but still —
            wanting nothing more
                than more
                    of each other

You sleep
so beautifully
nestled in clouds
fingers curled up
mouth softly smiling
to wondrous dreams

There are billions of stars
   with dozens of planets
     and handfuls of moons surrounding them

There are a trillion comets

There are supernova explosions
   and new planets being formed

Maybe there are countless peoples out there
   or maybe we're alone,
       I don't know

But I know one thing for sure:

There is nothing
   in the universe
      like you

It's nights like these
    twinkling twilight up above
        our tangled forms
    pointing out the constellations
      and making our own
    talking in dreams
      and letting ourselves wonder

What we will be
    when we crumble
        into stardust

    and hoping
    that we'll still be
      together

Your fingertips
    traced along my scars
    in search of the pain
    which lies just beneath the surface
    ready to tear through the skin

And maybe
    you knew then
    you were the only thing
    keeping my broken life stitched together

I want to nestle
   into the nook of your armpit
   and breathe in the scent of your chest
I want to see the world with you
   from our window
I want to watch the sun fall from the sky,
   the twinkling twilight light up the night
I want to trace the snowflakes
   that gather on our windowsill
   and draw you near when the cold
   creeps through
I want to see the tree leaves turn
   from green to brown to bare
   and back into bloom again
I want to see the rays of light
   tracing our plants along the walls
   in shadow
I want to wrap our bodies up close
   in soft blankets and warm skin
I want to let our minds wander together
   telling stories
   recalling memories
   painting dreams
   and our lips drawing together
I want to stay here forever

I grow weary of the days we spend apart
   the cold in my heart from each goodbye
   the silence that fills your laughless air
   the tapping of moth wings against
      the windows in all the empty rooms
   the sleep that fills the time between
      each of our meetings

One Hundred Days & One Night

I waited one hundred days
　　for one night
　　to spend eternity with you

And in that one night
　　everything changed between us
　　everything became more
　　everything became better
　　than it ever could've been before

And now, I can never go back
　　to the life I used to live
　　because the rest of the world
　　　is nothing like the taste
　　　　　　the touch
　　　　　　the smell
　　　　　　of the moon

We begin and end
　　only ever at night
　　　in the darkness
　　　in the twilight hour

When the rest of the world sleeps
　　we lie awake
　　between the sheets
　　and beneath the stars

Your lips spoke my name
and I came into being

in a way
I had never been before

It feels so good
to be here with you
It feels good
to be me

It feels like I belong here
where I should have
always been

LOVE BY NIGHT

Tempers flare
Anger bubbles up from my
stomach to my mouth –
the searing words burn my tongue
waiting to spew out on you

a moment of silent frustration
sits thick in the air

your scowl softens

the words on my tongue
fall back and become a ball in my throat

together, we manage
"I'm sorry."

There are some days I sound like a jerk
or you say something that makes me
                    feel stupid

but when we stop and slow down
and remember to lay down our knives
    and put down our defenses
we talk through it all and always seem
                to make it work

I would take every day with you
even the ones when we fight
over days spent feeling numb and empty
because often when we fight, it's because
    we care so much
    and sometimes we can't find
        the right words

LOVE BY NIGHT

There will still be those days
     the voice in the back of your head
          makes you feel small
               and takes you over

Those days
     you want to run away
          to push me away
          to cry those tears
               and strike yourself

We will work through these days
                    together

I will be with you
     to make sure my voice
     is louder than the lies
          you may tell yourself

          lies like "you're not good enough"
          because you are
               and you'll always be

Find me
in that dark place
you're spiraling toward

I'm a dim light
a faint glimmer
a starlight
but I'm down here with you

Find me
and come back to yourself
I'm here with you

When you're cold
  I'll wrap my arms around you
When you fall down
  I'll help you back up again
When your heart is broken
  I'll show you how to put it back together
When you feel alone
  I'll watch the sun come up beside you
When your eyes are filled with tears
  I'll kiss them away
When it feels like everyone has left you
  I'll be here
            Walking with you
            into the darkness

You Are More

You are more
    than the word beautiful –
    which was made to describe someone
      far simpler than you

You are more
    than this world
    has to offer

You are more
    than I could ever deserve
    to be with

You do not think you are enough
    but you are wrong –
    you are more than you know
      and more than enough

A life without the moon
is a life without light
            in darkness

It is unbearable
and frightening
and filled with terror

But a life with the moon
    is a life filled
      with beauty
      and wonder
      and love

There will be better days than these, my love

When we will stay in late
   and cuddle up close for hours on end
maybe we will go for a long drive
   through the mountains and the woodlands
   to pebbled shores
   where I can teach you to skip stones again
   and we'll trace each other's palms
      as we sing songs or read books
         on the drive home

but we'll go home together
   and put on a movie
   so we can pause it every couple minutes
   to talk about ourselves
   and each other
maybe we'll grow anxious
and want to stretch our legs
   and so we'll stroll the streets by sunset
      arm in arm together
      as the cold night nears
      and we'll point out the houses
         we want to live in

There will be better days, my love

she's that little ray of sunshine
she's that spring in my step
she's that glass of wine
    at the end of a long day
she's that gas pedal to the floor
she's that beginning to a new day
she's that song you can't help
    but sing along to
she's that bed of warm clean sheets
she's that summer when school gets out
she's that smile you just can't hide

I can't see too far ahead

I don't know if someday
I'll have a great big house with many rooms
   or just a little house
   a little bigger than a room
I don't know if I'll want
   one kid or two – or maybe none at all
I don't know if I'll work this job forever
   or if my fondness for it will wither away
I don't know if here is where
   I want to grow old
   or if my restless bones
   will seek somewhere new
I don't know if all my words
   will take me anywhere
   or if you'll be the only one
   who reads them
I don't know a lot of things
   but there is one thing I know for certain:
      through all these times
      and all these choices –
      some are mine, some made for me –

I know that I want you with me

Soft and warm
tingles rippling down my spine
sudden and unexpected
   but soothing

Kisses like raindrops

Bare and vulnerable
   beneath the moonlight

Fingers trembling
heartbeat racing
and lips quivering

you took my hand
   in yours

you whispered
something sweet

and I took you

Like a television left on
    far too long
    with the picture burned in,
I can still taste your lips
                        on mine

    You make it so hard
        to do anything
                        at all
            but think
                thoughts of you

Running my fingers
    through your hair
reading the pages to you

while you drift off into dreams

    I hope you're exploring new lands
        running barefoot over beaches

"Goodnight"
   you say to me
   as you close your eyes
"I will see you soon."

And it's true
   as soon as I close my eyes
   there you are
   in my dreams.

Who Goes First?

We had too much to drink that night
she fell asleep long before me

She danced in her dreams
and kicked at my knees

I smiled sleeplessly
as she tossed and turned
and softly moaned
tangled up in lucid fantasies

I watched her
and wished I could be there too,
where we are forever

And though I think she was sleeping
her hand sprang out and clutched
my fingers

She pulled me in
and I nestled up close

and fell into the darkness
to find her

Swallowed up in the dark
I love you in the night

I'll find your fingers
and trace your shape
and remember your form
  in light

We'll go on –
  journey deeper still
    into the dreaming

  Beyond the land we know
    so well

  And there, bid goodbye
    to reason and
    to meaning

You & I

Before it all began
   there was an explosion
     of light
     and matter
       in every direction

We saw cities rise and fall
   animals and humans alike
     being born
     growing up
     growing old
     and dying

And we saw ourselves
   suckling babies
   pimply teens
     always incomplete
       without each other

And then we met
   and there was an explosion
     of light
     and love
     and matter

I wonder if we met as children
  would you have chased me
    around the playground
    professing your love
    and picking me lilies?
  would I have noticed you
    or let you kiss me on the cheek?
  would I have been embarrassed
    or ashamed
    or would I be the one
        chasing you?

I wonder if we would still end up here

There is you
and there is me
    We are not together
      but there's a place where we are
      and sometimes I go there

I bring you lilacs
  and you greet me on the porch steps
    with kisses
  and we talk about our days
    by the fire
  and when our lips grow tired

  you run your fingers through my hair
  and I work the knots out of your shoulders
    and kiss your neck
    and tell you

You deserve to be kissed
    every day
    every moment

I've had this dream before
and I'll have it again

I'm back in these places I try to forget
People there laughing at me and I can't
                    shut them out
I run and I run and I can't run away
   but your hand is there to find my own
   your words are gentle in my ears
   and I feel them in my soul
   it's only a dream
   but you are with me
   and I realize now that it's okay –
                 it's all I need
I can turn back and face them
I can be here with you

Healing is
    being in the quiet and the darkness
    with the soft glow of the blazing fireplace
    and your arms wrapped around

    A book in my hands
    and soothing words falling from my lips
    our heavy eyes pulling us back

    The storm outside
    thunder booming and crackling overhead
        and the insistent patter of droplets
        the groan and grate of the wind
            tearing between the trees
                all of these sounds
                and I hear none of them

Healing is
        here

Linger a few minutes longer
with me in this dark space
help me forget all the things
I need to do today
with just your embrace

I feel the sunlight creeping across the sheets
but I want to hold the dark
where I can be whomever I want to be
    instead of what they want to make me
please, keep me here
stay with me

Explore these freckles of light
  with your gentle fingertips

      Find the unseen lines
          drawing them to each other
          across the nothing

Fill each silence with a smile
  or, if you must,
      interrupt it with a kiss

////////////////

Honeybee

I remember your lips
  when I kissed you

You became a hummingbird
  and you zipped and zoomed about
  the flitting of swift little wings
    tickled at my ears

And you sped away from me
  but I chased after
    shouting out – "but I love you"
  but you kept on and on,
        fluttering away
          until you were a tiny dot

        and then you came back
        only you weren't a bird
        no, you were a honeybee
        and your sound was a buzz
      and it scared me
        but I stayed still
        and you stung me

          but I smiled at you sweetly

Seeker in the dark
you find me where I don't belong
in my own indecision and self-doubt
and take me to a place
far better than I ever deserved

where I can plant small seeds
that could blossom into tomorrows
if I am clever and kind enough
to nourish them

sometimes I lose the way
please, show me the path
when I lose it

There was smoke rising up to the clouds
   between our tender fingertips
the lilacs at your feet
   tickled your nose
   with the smell of a smile
your kind little eyes held me up
   to some cloud I had never
   imagined myself on
I could turn to the sun at my back
   and see my future from here
   and my past as well, waving fondly
     as though hoping I still remember it

that sweet summer night we fell in love
   in the dreaming dew-dropped grass

The sheets open up
and I fall down down down
down deep inside

I'm awake
but my eyes refuse to open up —
they see no reason

I want to crumple up into a ball
and be thrown away
like a half-finished poem
not good enough to complete

there you find me
and unravel the crushed edges
to flatten me out
and read every line
and maybe even help me
fill out the rest

I remember you
from a time long before we met

when the light had not yet peeled
   the darkness back from the world

shapeless souls in the tumbles of emptiness
I remember the way our forms kissed
and the marks you left on my spirit
stayed upon me
when I felt my way into this body

I kiss you now and remember you
I've always known you
I remember

Travelers

We were old there
   skin folded loosely over frail bodies
   paper-thin bones ready to break
                 to a sudden gust
   and our fingers trembled against our will
     not out of fear, but because our bodies
       defied us

   But I remember
     one thing remained the same
     and it was the only way we seemed
       to recognize each other –
        our eyes

And then we were young
   nestled up against each other
   only soft and far away sounds –
   the gentle flitting of feathers in flight
   and the croak of the wind
     between the branches
   steady breathing and hearts tap-tapping
    yours or mine
      those eyes
            distant oceans

we weren't here
    but there –
    somewhere I have never been
    surrounded by the lapping of seafoam
      the caw of chittering gulls
        coarse and still soft sand
          heating against our skin
      the hammock swaying us
        with the tide
        I focused on your cold fingers

We were cold
  but warm against each other
    huddling tight beneath blankets
      as the flurries of snowy summer
        tickled at our cheeks
      and frosted the grass tips
Our arms fanned out
  making the angels
  we might someday become
Our eyes against the heavens
  defying the promise
    of winter's bitter kiss
Our eyes were closed
  but the worlds we saw
    in each other...

We took with us

The sun slipped away beneath the horizon
slivers of light faded
we walked the length of the beach
and lay there together in the dark
to watch the waves reaching toward us
and I realized I felt more bare
and vulnerable than I ever had before

and yet, I felt safer, too,
in the dark beneath the moon
with the rest of the world at our feet

I am a dreamer
  a starry-eyed child
  dipped in moonlight
  who climbs up mountains
  and sleeps in clouds

LOVE BY NIGHT

I can feel his hands upon me
from my shoulders down my spine
massaging away my worries
knots I've held up over time
he presses me – smooths me –
until I am made new
my neck falls loose like a noodle
my head grows heavy
   my feet are weary
   but then he finds those instead
   between my toes and around my heel
   he works and moves
   and twists and soothes
   my eyes grow sleepy
     and contentedly, I fall to sleep

Sweet dreams
my little tosser
my little turner
my little sleep walker,
      sleep talker
my little angel,
  fanning your body out across the bed
my little cloud skipper
my little star sailor
my little moonbeam

I want you to close your eyes
   and let me pick you up in my arms
   and take you out to my car in the snow
   and kiss you
   and sing to you
     until you fall asleep

And when you wake up
   I want to kiss you
   and carry you out
   and lay you down in the sand

The water will splash your toes
   and it will be warm
   and it will surprise you
   and I'll kiss you
   and I'll kiss you
   and I'll kiss you until you wake

We left the shore behind,
   drifting on the gentle waves,
   lapping water at our sides

The clouds rolled out
   across the water in billowing curtains

I took your hand in mine
   and looked into your eyes

The moon shone on the horizon
   and all the night sky
   looked down on us with grace

The world fell away
   on this night
    and all that remained of it —
           was our love

The lights were all on – even the lamps
she was staring down at me
sitting cross-legged on my chest
poking my cheeks

"Our boat is about
to disembark –
wake up!"
she said

And I did

to find her sleeping
soundly beside me
murmuring softly to herself –
or maybe to me –

"Don't forget your pants."

Captain of the Sleepless Voyage

O my little Calypso
   sprawled out across the sheets
   sunk into deep visions of beyond
   her swirling wispy breaths
     rippling white silken water
       stretched taut beneath our forms

Yet these fingers plod on –
   tracing over linen waves
   exploring moonlit speckled skin
     bare and rhythmic against the night

And I gaze upon her tightly kept lids
   holding back
     orbs of azure waters
     uncharted lands beyond

      It is far too late
       but not yet early enough
        for waking

      And so I sail on

I can see the sea
  in your blue eyes

I can taste the salt
  from your tears
    on my lips

I can hear the waves
    softly falling against the shore
    with my ear
      pressed to your chest

and I can feel the water
  all around me
  slipping through
    on its way to you

We left our bodies hours ago

    swimming naked among the cosmos
    constellations stretched overhead
      like the string lights on our porch
    eyes brimming with forevers
    lips spelling love in every way we know
                      how to

here, we are free
and though the gentle twilight is fading,

    I don't want to go back

Imagine our lives unfolding –
   playing out like little Super 8 movies
     in a million different ways

Maybe we stay here or move far away
Maybe somewhere they speak our language
     or maybe somewhere they don't
Maybe we'll have a little home
     or maybe a castle
Maybe we'll grow old together
     or maybe we'll have a couple kids
Maybe we'll have two girls with your eyes
     and my smile
   or maybe we'll try for them
     and find out we can't
Maybe we'll make it big
     or maybe we will stay this way –
      our only happiness is each other
Maybe the film will go on forever
     or run out before we're ready
      for it to end

Every film is beautiful
   and I'd live them all
     with you

Star kid,
lay down your head
don't be afraid of the dark
journey deep into dreams
stay wild and wondrous
grow up gently
and don't forget
to look up at the moon
when you've grown too old to run

When I go
lay me down
against the earth
where my heart can beat
with the beat of the mother
who bore me from her branches
who shaped me from dirt and bones
who will shape the next from my own
take me home

I'm not ready for the end
   not when I feel
   I've only just begun with you

I want to see what we will become

I want to see the choices we will make
   together
I want to tell them all about us,
   to shout it from the rooftops

I want to get lost in you
   and forget about
     life and death –
      beginnings and end

I want to feel our love
          forever

LOVE BY NIGHT

We crawl beneath
the thick silk sheets of the night sky,
swimming boundless,
bodies tumbling and weightless,
with only each other's form to guide our way
  through the dark

We are alone here, in this place

Just the two of us,
    the moon and the stars

I would love to spend eternity
  exploring the depths with you
    just the two of us
      and millions of miles
        of places to go

A Reception Beneath the Stars

We were out on this big boat somewhere
  and it was the middle of the night

I saw us dressed up
  in our nicest clothes
  in clothes far better
    than anything either of us
      has ever owned

And there was the smoothest
  sultry jazz band playing
  music straight from their soul

We held each other close
our other hands wrapped around
  flutes of bubbly champagne
  sweet notes tickling our noses

We danced with such reckless joy
  and wore smiles that
  overlooked our fancy clothes

    I stared at you and wondered
      if I was dreaming
        and you kissed me
        awake

Whenever I wake up
next to you

it feels like
coming home

Your hands are cozy autumn evenings
   sitting fireside in sweaters
   while the leaves fall outside

Your kisses are early spring dewdrops
   from last night's gentle rain
   blossoming beauties from deep within

Your heartbeat is a warm summer day
   wild and full of a youthful energy
   to soak our basking bodies beneath the sun

Your eyes are merry winter songs
   singing wordless over the chill
   of the promise of the long winter night

I won't always have the words
   to pull you back from the dark

   but I will always be here
     to sit with you in it
     and take your hand
     or wrap my arms around you
     until it passes

for every day of sunshine
   there will be a night of darkness

     but I want to spend both of them
      with you

I will be careful with you
  but I promise to be reckless too

I will be thoughtful in words
  but also passionate in action

I will know when to follow
  but lead when you don't know the way

I will hold you close
  but if you ever tell me to leave,
    I'm sorry but it's something
                      I'll never do

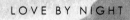

Storm Shelter

There will be long gloomy days
full with storm clouds and claps of thunder
the wind will howl and
the dogs will whimper
lightning will tear apart the sky
  but we will be safe
    with each other
      and we will know
        every storm will pass

We hid out in old abandoned houses
  protected by crumbling fences

  We went wherever they weren't –
wherever we could be together

  We stayed a night in a castle
     a day in a haunted house
    and a few dozen
       huddled up together
      surrounding ourselves
       with blankets and cardboard

Oh, but we were so happy
  and I wouldn't take back
    a single day

Things I'm grateful for:
- My life and health
- The family I have – including the friends
- Great food and refreshing drinks
- Sunsets and sunrises
- The stars and the moon
- The sea and the wild
- Soft blankets and softer cuddles
- Good books
- You

I never knew I liked grocery shopping
    until I pushed the cart around with you
I never knew I liked mornings
    until we shared some tea and smiles
I never knew I liked cooking
    until we made it more than just a meal
I never knew I liked hosting
    until I saw how we work as a team
I never knew I liked reading with someone
    until we burned through some books
    together

I never know what I'll discover next
with you
    but I can't wait to find out

LOVE BY NIGHT

One of our favorite things to do together
is walk the streets
and point out the houses we pass
to talk about the wonder
of what living there would be like

How old do you think that house is?

That place has nice bones, but it's
  definitely a fixer-upper

Those stairs are fine now
  but when we're old –

That arch over the front door
The color of the roof
The garden you could plant
I love the cut of that fencing

Someday, my love
we will have a place of our own

Whatever happens
I know it will always be like this

the same page that we are on
the healthy way we communicate
the flow and vibe that we bring
the groove that we cook with or clean
the way that we share everything
   with each other
            even the hard stuff
            but especially the love –
               the love we have for things
                       for people
                       for each other

            whatever happens
            I know
            it will always be like this

I will always remember our first house
    our upside-down doorknob
    our hall lights that never worked
    our unfixable faucet
    our warm refrigerator
    our windy recycling days
    our power outages

    our first carpet and couch
    our brisk morning walks around the block
    our cozy movie nights
    our paintings on the walls
    our game nights we'd host
    our delicious home-cooked meals
    our lazy days in bed
    our little needy dog

Wherever we go from here
    I will take this place with me

We'll paint the world across the walls
   and we'll start here
   where we grew up

We'll stretch our arms out wide
   mark every place we want to drive
   we'll push pins in the places
   and take a drive together
   to replace some of those pins
     with memories

We'll name the places far away from us –
   the places we've only ever dreamed of
   and someday we'll save up the money
   and cross the oceans instead
     to press our fingers against
     this soil in distant lands
     instead of the images in our minds

We'll go there – wherever we can
   we have our whole lives to get there
   together

I look forward to a few things
    the notes you leave in my lunchbox
    the way you flick the porch light
        on and off
        as I back out the driveway
    the "I love you" text you send me
        as I drive away
    the soft snores you sing
        while I read you to sleep
    the way you fall into my arms
        when I return home to you
        in the morning
    the steaming cups of coffee we sip
        as we meet at this place in between –
        me about to fall sleep
        and you, just barely waking up
    the days we count down together
        to the weekend ahead
            when our worlds align once more

these passing moments
    are all that get me through

I remember the feeling of
   your lips on my cheek
   our feet against the warm beach
   the waves lapping at our ankles
   your heart beating soft and tranquil
   the wind through my hair
darling, take me back there

Meals

There will be breakfasts in bed
    I'll put the coffee on and give you just a
    splash of cream – until your coffee looks
                         caramel
there will be nice dinners
    we'll get dressed up real nice and go out
    somewhere that costs more than it should
    but we'll go there like we belong –
    we'll know what we deserve
there will be takeout nights
    you'll get the silverware and the plates
    set up on the coffee table while I take
    our order from the delivery driver
there will be picnics in the grass
    we'll lay out a blanket and snack
    on the fruits of our labor –
    holding each other close and just
    being there in that moment together

there will be all kinds of meals
    and they will all be a part of us –
    an important part
        that we'll always share *together*

On days when work is too stressful,
when my self-discipline is nonexistent,
when I'm too tired to even feel human,

you smile, you make me laugh a little,
you help me keep perspective.

When I feel anxious and depressed,
unsuccessful and like a big lazy blob,

you motivate me, you encourage me,
you make feel capable, strong, and
altogether lovely.

I know these bad days will never go away.
Being with the love of my life doesn't
mean a happily-ever-after every day.

But it does mean the bad days aren't
as frequent.

It does mean I feel stronger to fight
for my happiness.

It means you make me love myself
a little bit more.

A Letter to Future Us

We want you both to keep looking forward
    to the days to come – to the days
    and nights you'll spend together

We want you to experience new things
    every year until your last

We want you to keep your hearts open
    to each other – to keep sharing the things
    you love, to share new things you discover

We want you to share things with each other
    that are sometimes hard to talk about

We want you to look at us here and know
    we're happy – and we hope you never
    lost this

We hope you still look at each other
    with those alluring eyes –
    with tender searching hands
      and forgiving lips
      and kind, listening ears

We hope the distance between us here
    and you there
    is long and full of adventure

We want you both to be happy
   with who you have become
   and the marks you've left on hearts –
   and we hope they are tender impressions
   rather than scars

We want you to know it is okay
   that you've made mistakes
   because we know you both have

We want you to know you did enough
   and you are enough
   and we are proud –
   don't look back at this time
     or the time between then and now
                with regret

We want you to remember
   it is never too late to change –
                not even now

We love you both
   and we love that you found each other
   that you found someone to show you
   everything you deserve

You are the sun in the day
  and the moon in the night

You brighten my life
  and if I ever forget
    I just have to look up at the sky
      and know that there's a you
        who loves me

You are the moon
  always shining
  always there for me
    even when I can't see you

You rise at night
  and gently kiss the world

  And even the dark sides of you
    are beautiful

Sometimes I am scared
because I don't know what comes next
    a ring
    a question
    a house
    a couple kids
Where do we go?
Does this fun just disappear –
    this me and this you?
    these people we are now will be no more
    I see ourselves shrinking and scrambling
    out the door

    how do we still be ourselves?
    how do we hold on to everything we are?

Whenever the time comes
if ever the time comes

I hope I can be a good father

I am so scared of messing it up
   of making someone like me

I will read our kid to sleep
   and let them leave the light on
   if they need it

I will let them be whomever
   they want to be

I hope they don't feel the pressure
   but I hope they're better than me

I hope they know no matter what they do
   I will be proud of them

I used to not want to be a mother
    and that's something
    you just don't tell people

Now I can see how that life could be
    and I'm starting to want it for myself

I want to give that kind of love
    to someone else –
        I have so much of it to spare

Maybe it never felt right before
    but with you now
        it does

It is fun to pick out names
to imagine what little quirks
or facial features
or skills they will pick up from us
to wonder who they will become
and how we will raise them
or the ways we will love them

it is fun to wonder
to think of what could be
if we decide we want to maybe
                 expand our little family

When the old bones break
when the hair falls from my head
when the body grows frail
    and fades to dust,
my love will remain

I remember when
you said,

    "Promise me,
    if we become more than this,
    we won't lose this.
    I don't ever want to lose
    our friendship
    even if we're more than friends."

And I know some days
move faster than others
and that was so many days ago
but you're still
my best friend
and I never want that to change either

You still make me feel invincible
you still help me find the stars in the dark
   and the moon in the day
you still make me smile and laugh
   and remind me that everything
     will be okay
you still help me find the words
   when I can't find my voice
you still speak up for me
   when I feel like I don't have a choice
you still make me want to be better
   but you also still remind me
     that I'll always be enough

When I grow old,
 I will find a new way
  each day
 to tell you why I love you
When I grow old,
 I will still laugh at your dumb jokes
When I grow old,
 I will still take your hand when
 you're staring off
When I grow old,
 I will still take out the trash
  and wash the dishes
When I grow old,
 I will still read you to sleep
When I grow old,
 I will still look at you with wonder
  at how I ever tricked you to be mine

I don't know quite
    how many days, or months, or years
        I have left
    but I want to spend every last one
        with you

here's to the days to come
here's to the days we've had

here's to everything we will be
    whatever it is
        I know for sure
    it's made better with you

Lines

I wish I could draw a single straight line
    starting from here
    back to where we first began
    and all along the memories in between

But there were other lines too –
the lines of your face my fingers traced over
the lines we waited in while we
                    joked and giggled
the lines we gave them to make them think
                we weren't us
the lines we used to hang our clothes on
the lines we threw to hoist each other up
            when we were down
the lines we wrote when words weren't
              enough
the lines we crossed when we knew
          we loved each other
the lines painted on the road passing by as
    I looked out the passenger-side window
      while you drove us through the night to
    anywhere we could forget everything but
           each other

172

I remember when you wrote me 365 reasons
   why you love me – to open one every day

I remember when I wrote you
a book of poems
   just for you – to read when you miss me

I remember when we first sang together
   and when we first read together

I remember when I met you and learned
your name
   and how you looked
   and how you looked at me

I remember our first tickle fight together
   and how we stared at each other when I
   pinned you

I remember the first time
we cried on each other
   and how it felt to be held by you

I remember the last time I saw you
   and the next time is too far away
            but I'll remember it too

Things I'm looking forward to:
- The day we tie our hearts together
- Whisking away somewhere with you
- Making a home with you
- Cooking and dancing
- More tickle fights
- Late night talks until the sun comes up
- The rest of my days and nights with you

Okay, my dear, everything is okay
I am with you
and everything will be alright
I know how weary you've grown
but it's time to lay it all down

Come here
come into my arms
let my fingers remind you that you are safe
and my lips remind you that you are loved
and let's forget about it all

Let me take you away
lay your head back
    against my chest
let me take you somewhere better
    somewhere that deserves you

We've spent so many days
holed-up together
in this space
just big enough for two –
that's right, just me and you

but there's no other space
I'd rather be

when we get let out
I will go wherever you go
and together we'll be free
to walk the empty streets
or sail off into the sea

Do you know
the places I would go with you?

We could brave the cold wild of Scandinavia
or lie beside the sunny seashores of Hawaii
we could dance the Bourbon Street
                              of New Orleans
or take to the slippery gondolas of Venice
we could kiss beneath the twinkling
                              Eiffel Tower
or learn the lush ways of the Amazon

we could go anywhere, my love

My Dreams for the Future

I hope we will always find joy
   in the little things
   and that we will be kind –
      to each other, to others, and to ourselves

I hope that when we fight
   we find a way to make it work
     and make it better again

I hope we never stop
   making each day special
    and full of wonder

I hope we remember
   as happy as we make each other
    it's okay to cry sometimes too

I hope the days without you
   pass by quicker
    than the days we spend together

I hope we never forget our dreams
   or stop looking to the night sky
    for wonder
      or love
        or each other

I hope we keep calling each other
  our names we've made for one another
    instead of the ones our parents gave us

I hope if we choose to be parents
  we are good ones
    and we raise our children
      to be loving and open

I hope even when we grow old and weary
  we do not become
    bitter or angry

I hope whether we are rich or poor
  we will always find enough
    in each other
      and in ourselves

I hope we never forget
  the big important things
    or the little ones either
      like pillow forts
      or dancing in the kitchen –
        all the things that made us
          along the way

And last of all
  I hope that at the end
    we will still be us

There were those nights
  we stayed up until the morning talking

    We watched the sunset
      and the sunrise

and it felt like time
  was irrelevant

These days, we read each other to sleep

  and wait for each other
    in our dreams

I know
    some days the world will be far too heavy
      on your shoulders

So let me carry it
    with you

We'll sing songs
    while we walk into forever

When you go
come find me
up in the stars

I'll be waiting for you there

Thank you for reading this book.
You can view more of our work together on Instagram
@skwilliamspoetry and Twitter @skwilliamspoet.

Feel free to write to us!

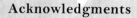

Acknowledgments

to all our followers and supporters on social
media, from those who have been there since
the beginning to those just finding us now

to Sabrina & Terry, for their endless support
and Laurie for spreading our words

to Gregg & Christie, Shannon & Steve,
Sue & Ron, Carli, and Brandon, for their
constant encouragement and love

to Piper, the best dog we could ever ask for

to Karissa, Vince & Sarah, Stefanie, Mallory,
Oscar, and all the friends who cared enough
to be a part of our journey

to the incredibly talented Justin Estcourt,
for his beautiful cover artwork – find more
of his art on his Instagram @jetsyart

to James, Courtney, and Wilder, for their
help in making our dream become a reality

and to everyone at Andrews McMeel, who
took a chance on us and believed in us